The
Modernist
Home

First published by V&A Publications, 2006
V&A Publications
Victoria and Albert Museum
South Kensington
London SW7 2RL

Distributed in North America by Harry N. Abrams, Inc., New York

ISBN-10 1851774769
ISBN-13 9781851774760
Library of Congress Control Number 2005935060

10 9 8 7 6 5 4 3 2 1
2010 2009 2008 2007 2006

Designed by Holmes Wood
New V&A photography by Christine Smith, V&A Photographic Studio

Front jacket illustration: Le Corbusier and Pierre Jeanneret, Villa Savoye, 1928–31. See pp.10–11.
Photo: Tim Benton
Back jacket illustration: Poul Henningsen, table lamp. Nickel-plated brass, Bakelite, aluminium and
white opalescent glass. 1928. V&A: M.26:1-5-1992. See p.58
Frontispiece: Le Corbusier and Pierre Jeanneret, Villa Savoye, 1928–31. Photo: Tim Benton

Printed in Hong Kong

V&A Publications
Victoria and Albert Museum
South Kensington
London SW7 2RL
www.vam.ac.uk

The Modernist Home

Tim Benton

V&A Publications

LEFT
J.J.P. Oud,
Design for Blijdorp
Municipal Housing.
1931–2.
Watercolour,
pencil and silver.
Nederlands
Architectuurinstituut,
Rotterdam © DACS 2005

Introduction

In 1939, the illustrator and acute observer of the English home, Osbert Lancaster, recorded a radio programme for the BBC. Preserved on a scratchy 78rpm disk, Lancaster, in his almost impenetrable cut-glass tones, laid out his argument, guaranteed to offend both Modernists and Classicists alike.

The 'Modern Movement in architecture' was nothing less than a rerun of the neo-Gothic revival, he claimed. Like the Goths, the Modernists had prophets (Pugin, Le Corbusier), evangelists (Ruskin, Gropius) and high priests (Morris, Mies van der Rohe). The Modern Movement, therefore, was best understood as a religion or sect, rather than in the rational terms in which it was normally presented.

As usual, Lancaster got the essentials right, even if the detail was a bit off-beam. Modernism as a belief structure passed through an early phase of heart-searching and criticism, dipped into a tornado of wild prophecy and idealism after World War I, to emerge around 1925 in Holland, France and Germany as an international cult with a reforming mission to change the world. In the next 15 years, the movement spread like wildfire through Europe and the Americas, without ever acquiring full official recognition and with its full share of martyrs and heretics. In 1945, Modernism emerged as the state religion in most countries, generally referred to by this stage as the International Style, where it flourished for 20 years before collapsing into the wit, scepticism and agnosticism of post-Modernism.

Osbert Lancaster used a term common in Anglo-Saxon parlance: the 'Modern Movement'. The word 'Modernism' is a term borrowed from post-war art criticism to lump together a set of ideas and practices. What these ideas and practices were will emerge throughout the course of the book.

LEFT
'Twentieth Century Functional' in
Osbert Lancaster,
Pillar to Post 1938

Art and Life: 'house' and 'home'

The title of this book, *The Modernist Home*, might be considered a contradiction in terms. Many houses are works of architecture without possessing those qualities associated with a 'home'. Was it possible to design a Modernist 'house' which was also recognizably a 'home'? The house exhibited by Mies and Lilly Reich at the Berlin Building Exhibition in 1931 is undoubtedly a sophisticated and elegant piece of design, but it looks as much like a bank as a home. In fact, this model house was based on a building intended to represent Germany at the International Exhibition in Barcelona in 1929. Its only function was to provide room for two chairs and a table at which the King and Queen of Spain could sign the visitors' book.

The Barcelona Pavilion designed by Mies consists of chromium-plated cross-shaped stanchions supporting a roof slab, interspersed with walls of alabaster, marble and glass which do not actually meet up to enclose the interior. And yet this is a kind of house; the 1931 model house shows how it might be adapted for human use.

LEFT
Mies van der Rohe,
Barcelona Pavilion, 1929;
reconstructed 1981–6
Photo: Tim Benton
© DACS 2005

ABOVE
Mies van der Rohe
and Lilly Reich,
model house
exhibited at the
Berlin Building
Exhibition.
From *Wasmuths
Monatshefte*, 1931

RIGHT
Le Corbusier and
Pierre Jeanneret,
salon of Villa
Savoye, 1928–31
Photo: Tim Benton
© FLC/ ADAGP,
Paris and DACS,
London 2005

Le Corbusier's Villa Savoye, a weekend villa designed for a wealthy couple and their teenage son, is almost as abstract as the Barcelona Pavilion. Even when it was occupied by the Savoye family, the few items of furniture could not make this luminous space 'homey'. As in a Palladian villa, you had to appreciate the architectural values of space and light, colour and texture to find satisfaction in a house like this.

Modernism has often been represented as inhuman and artificial, a soulless and mechanistic approach to life. Terms such as 'functionalism', 'cubism' and 'nudism' were used and comparisons made with offices and factories. More recently, a strand in feminist writing has revived the idea that Modernism represented the imposition on home-based women of masculine values: over-rational, repressed and inhuman.

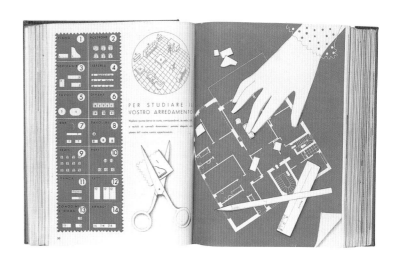

Woman as creator

In 1924, German architect Bruno Taut's little red book *The New Dwelling* was published with the subtitle 'Dedicated to woman as creator'. And in 1928, the French designer Paulette de Bernège, a specialist in domestic design, and especially the kitchen, wrote a book called *If Women Designed Houses...* Her view was that male architects had little relevant experience when allocating space and designing circulation in houses, condemning women to unnecessary strain and labour as a result. In the 1930s, the Italian magazine *Domus* frequently published plans of houses for its readers to pass on to builders to construct. Here again, the idea was that it was women who should lay out the interior.

It seems that architects, at least in the homes they design for others, seek above all the virtues of order, light, space and geometric harmony, and avoid clutter, confusion, dark corners and intimate spaces. Many of us will recognize in these oppositions tensions about how to live which go beyond gender difference. Modernism accentuated these tensions, striving for an aesthetic control of space and surface which many would consider intolerable.

LEFT
Domus, 'Per studiare il vostro arredamento',
1938

THE HOUSE THAT JACK BUILT

LEFT
Thomas Dalgleish
McLean, 'The house
that Jack built',
Daily Mail Ideal
Home Exhibition,
1931

LEFT
Mrs Phyllis Lee
and Douglas
Tanner, FRIBA,
'The house
that Jill built',
Daily Mail Ideal
Home Exhibition,
1930

Suspicion of architects was alive and well in the 1920s and 1930s. In 1929, the *Daily Mail* launched a competition to design a house. The catch was that only married women who were not architects could apply. The result, 'The house that Jill built', was constructed at the Ideal Home Exhibition in 1930. The following year it was the turn of married men, and 'The house that Jack built' turned out to be surprisingly Modernist.

The heroism of modern life

Perhaps the key to understanding the Modernist house is that it was not designed for just anyone. This was an art movement, intended for those who could understand and appreciate it. Comparing the house designed for the Bauhaus teacher László Moholy-Nagy with a photograph of the man and one of his factory-made artworks might support the hypothesis that Modernism was conceived in the image of a very particular kind of person.

It has to be said that most Modernist architects did envisage a new approach to living: more active and austere, less passive and comfortable. Comfort was not, perhaps, the most important thing in a world dominated by poverty and squalor; Modernist intellectuals and architects were on a mission to reflect this.

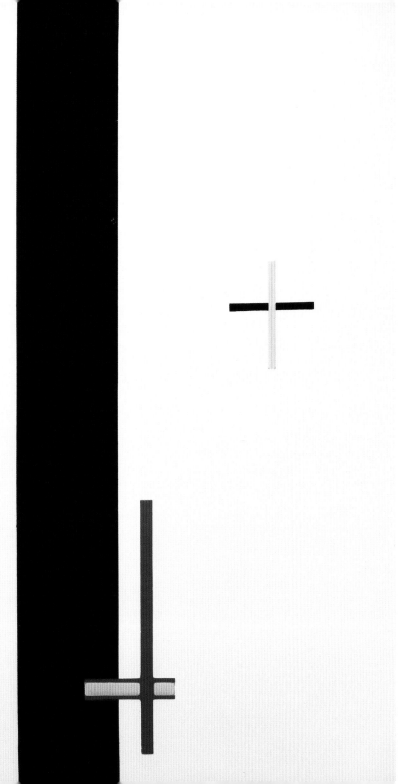

Modernism
and
Modernity

There is a distinction that needs to be made between 'Modernism' and 'modernity'. Modernity describes the way in which people understand a world changing rapidly under the influence of economic, technical and social influences. 'Modern' therefore means a little more than simply 'contemporary'. Although there has always been change, the nature of the transformation of society in the industrial nations during the twentieth century has been perceived differently than in previous times. Modernism was one kind of artistic response to modernity.

Another response to these changes was inevitable, gradual and irreversible. The typical house or apartment of 1945 might have looked fairly similar to that of 1918, but it would have benefited from instant hot water and electric lighting, enclosed WCs, separate bathroom and kitchen and a range of items of equipment, from the ubiquitous radio to the increasingly affordable washing machine and refrigerator. New materials provided better insulation against damp and cold. These changes made only gradual shifts in the domestic aesthetic: the Battle of Britain pilots cycled off to their Spitfires from cottages which may have had steel windows, but which probably also had tiled or thatched roofs and chintz curtains.

LEFT
Wells Coates, Ekco radio.
Bakelite.1934
V&A: W.23–1981

What is now referred to as Modernism derived from the particular perception of change during the 1920s and 1930s which deduced the need for a much more sudden and radical transformation in the appearance of houses and the objects within. The Modernist architect Wells Coates took a new phenomenon, such as the radio, and put it into a symbolically appropriate form: made of Bakelite for ease of production, circular to express the turning tuning dial. His radio can be described as a Modernist object because its form is expressive of modernity as well as incorporating new technology.

Similarly, Modernist houses express the structural potential of reinforced concrete or steel construction in ways which would be impossible in brick. Maxwell Fry's Sun House in north London is characteristically flat-roofed, with white walls, large expanses of glass and prominent over-hangs and balconies. The interiors of Modernist houses are typically opened out into wide spaces illuminated by large glass walls and windows, with the structure often separated from the walls through the use of thin concrete struts (*pilotis*).

Free-standing furniture is replaced by built-in fixtures which are ingeniously arranged to meet practical needs. Connell, Ward and Lucas's house at 66 Frognal, just a few feet from Fry's Sun House, is a typical example of Modernist interior design, with its neatly arranged built-in cupboards. Notice the adjustable electric light, the round ventilators to avoid condensation and the Ferranti fire installed in the wall on the left.

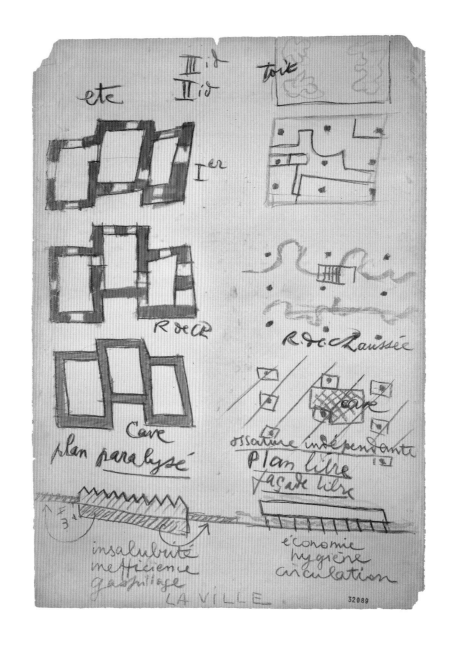

ete

II id
II id

toit

I er

R de Ch

R de Chaussée

Cave

plan paralysé

ossature indépendante

Plan libre

façade libre

insalubrité
inefficience
gaspillage

économie
hygiène
circulation

LA VILLE

32089

Modernist Ideas

Structural rationalism

The roots of Modernist architectural theory and practice stretch back into the nineteenth century. A long tradition of writing had emphasized the idea of structural rationalism. This had been the argument of neo-Gothic supporters of the Gothic style, in which a daring system of stone construction using flying buttresses and thin, tall piers obtained a maximum amount of light in the interior. The implication was that the arrival of steel and concrete as building systems should revolutionize architecture, just as the flying buttress had led to the Gothic style.

RIGHT
Le Corbusier and
Pierre Jeanneret,
dining room and living
room of Cook house,
Boulogne sur Seine,
1926–8
Photo: Tim Benton
© FLC/ ADAGP, Paris
and DACS, London 2005

LEFT
Le Corbusier, lecture
drawing: design of
a traditional house
and a modern
house on *pilotis*.
Pencil, charcoal
and pastel on card.
1929
© FLC/ ADAGP, Paris
and DACS, London 2005

LEFT
J.J.P. Oud,
Blijdorp municipal
housing, 1931–2
Watercolour,
pencil and silver.
Nederlands
Architectuurinstituut,
Rotterdam © DACS 2005

Le Corbusier explained these ideas in his lectures by drawing the 'paralyzed plan' of the traditional house, with the walls of each floor resting on those below, compared to the 'free plan' of the reinforced concrete house. Here, the thin concrete supports carry the structure, leaving the walls free for windows and making it possible to plan each floor with complete freedom. The house designed by Le Corbusier for the American journalist and painter William E. Cook and his French wife Jeanne exemplifies these principles precisely. The floor slabs are carried by slender *pilotis*, to allow for a window which stretches the full width of the house.

These ideas are further linked by the notion that only by industrializing the construction process could the daunting task of housing urban workers be achieved (typically in mass housing programmes). All the Modernist architects proposed designs for popular housing estates and derived the forms of their domestic architecture from the stark realities of mass housing. The Blijdorp housing project by J.J.P. Oud, the city architect of Rotterdam, is typical of this kind of work.

Functionalism

Structural rationalism and arguments of social utility could lead to theories of functionalism. The functionalist argument took one of two forms. Either it was argued that aesthetic value was a luxury in the face of the social tasks at hand, or, more dubiously, that anything that was well made and served its purpose would necessarily be beautiful. To understand functionalist statements you have to keep in mind that most of them were coined by artists and should be taken with a pinch of salt. The functionalist argument was difficult to get right. For example, in the English version of Bruno Taut's book *Modern Architecture*, he ends the chapter 'What is Modern Architecture?' with the functionalist statement: 'The aim of Architecture is the creation of perfect, and therefore also beautiful, efficiency' (Taut, p.9). In the German original, the word 'therefore' is lacking, and Taut certainly did not believe that what was functional must necessarily be beautiful.

les techniques sont
l'assiette même du lyrism

lyrisme =
création individuelle
drame, pathétique = rateur
eternelle

economique   standardisation   Tâcho
                    industrialisation   urgent
                    taylorisation
sociologique   un ple...

The zeitgeist

Another ingredient in the Modernist cocktail was the notion of the zeitgeist. The zeitgeist principle was that architects should assimilate the overall conditions of the time and create buildings accordingly. The catch was that architecture should never be seen to copy the material world too literally. Yet the tell-tale port-hole windows, marine railings and bridge-like projections of many Modernist designs gave modern architecture a bad name; Bruno Taut even published an image of a spoof villa derived directly from a photograph of the SS *Australia*.

The trick was to absorb rather than imitate modernity. Le Corbusier used an amusing sketch to express his view of the relationship between the material world and what he called 'lyricism'. It's like eating a three course dinner, he said. Once you've digested your economics, sociology and technology, you light your pipe and suddenly, like a little bird, imagination takes flight. The modern world should be a stimulation, not a straitjacket.

RIGHT
Sigfried Giedion,
suspended stairs
within the Eiffel
Tower, 1889
(connection from
the ground floor to
the first platform).
From Giedion,
*Building in
France* (1928)

'Interpenetration' and a new sense of space

Machines and works of engineering were among the most powerful stimuli for the Modernist imagination. The Swiss critic and historian Sigfried Giedion went so far as to compare an appreciation of the hidden structural realities of contemporary architecture to a kind of psychoanalysis of the modern world (exposing the repressed realities of modernity). He also found a way of aestheticizing the diaphanous steel structures of buildings such as the Marseilles Transporter Bridge or the Eiffel Tower in terms of what he called 'interpenetration'.

He believed that the essential experience of great engineering works was not their rationality but the giddy sense of vertigo when looking through the maze of girders, whose fragmentation of the world around created a sensation of space akin to that of Cubism. Similarly, walls conceived as glass membranes appeared to Giedion to allow inside and outside to blend together in a time-space continuum.

Modernist photographers attuned to this way of thinking sought ways to represent buildings as almost abstract plays of reflection and transparency. Moholy-Nagy produced unusual and disturbing images of the sense of space created by new structures and concluded his influential book *Von Material zu Architektur* (1928) with an image representing the future of architecture as he saw it. This was composed of two photographs of the recently completed Van Nelle factory near Rotterdam, printed in negative and superimposed. Only by these means, he thought, could the potential of the new transparent space be represented.

Furthermore, this spatial blurring could be likened to the radical social objective of breaking down the barriers defending middle class property. A Modernist house was spatially open and, at least symbolically, socially transparent. But these principles, when applied to houses, had unwanted side effects: large expanses of glass could lead to a sense of exposure. There is some truth to the 'nudity' slur of the opponents of Modernism. Most of us feel uncomfortably naked while standing before a glass wall, irrespective of whether there are actually people outside looking in. The studio designed by Le Corbusier for his friend Amédée Ozenfant might seem unbearably cold and puritanical, but you have to remember that both men were involved in the Purist art movement, which sought to reform modern art in the image of the machine and strived for universally valid geometric forms.

For many Modernists, the quintessential domestic pleasure was that of contemplating a fine view in pleasant surroundings. Le Corbusier preferred to use horizontal windows in domestic architecture. The bungalow he designed for his parents on Lake Geneva has a window running almost the length of the house and framing the view; Le Corbusier also liked to frame the view in open air settings.

The Modernist Client

In the early years of Modernism (1920–5), architects had little choice other than to dream of vast projects on paper and build small houses for friendly intellectuals. The modern house thus became a litmus test for modern architecture.

The artists, intellectuals and young professional couples who inhabited the Modernist house did not want the snug, cosy, satisfied homes of their parents. They wanted a dwelling as a launch pad for their active lifestyle, open to new ideas and free from convention and bourgeois restrictions. Sport, physical fitness and hygiene became an obsession with governments as well as individuals in the 1920s and 1930s. Max Burchartz's poster for a dance festival captures this enthusiasm and youthful exuberance in a Constructivist idiom. This too was part of the zeitgeist and came to be reflected in the domestic interior.

LE JARDIN COUVERT

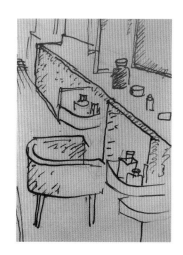

Often, demonstration Modernist dwellings were designed for sportsmen or sportswomen. The apartment designed by the Bauhaus student and teacher Marcel Breuer is replete with signs of modernity: nubile young women work out in a living space devoid of furniture, to the accompaniment of a gramophone.

To be a Modernist client was a declaration of faith, which sometimes paid dividends in promoting a career and making a public statement, but often brought the hapless victim to the brink of bankruptcy or beyond. Experimenting with new building techniques never comes cheap, and Modernist clients had to suffer a string of teething problems with condensation (caused by large expanses of glass), leaking roofs and stained, cracked or peeling walls.

Sometimes wealthy clients had to be coaxed into commissioning houses from Modernist architects. Le Corbusier developed a tactic of seducing his female clients with little sketches showing how their house would look. He shows the family inviting their friends to some amateur dramatics on the two-storey terrace; he shows the young woman's dressing table and breakfast awaiting her on the roof terrace looking out over the Parc St James in Paris. Invariably Modernist architects drew their houses drenched in sunlight, with life lived outdoors as well as indoors.

Another method of attracting clients was the display of artistic models or drawings in public exhibitions. Le Corbusier exhibited large plaster models of his houses in the Salon d'Automne in Paris between 1922 and 1924. The Citrohan model was a prototype mass-produced concrete house, to be manufactured like an automobile – a Ford or a Citroën. The coloured axonometric of the Cook house is an example of a beautifully rendered drawing which could impress the client and be published in an art journal. Designing houses was not just a question of pleasing the client, but of advancing the architect's career.

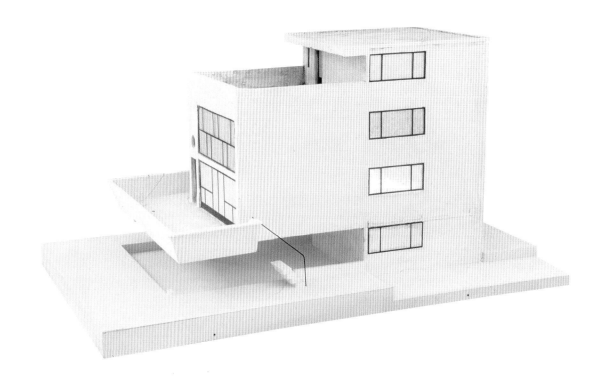

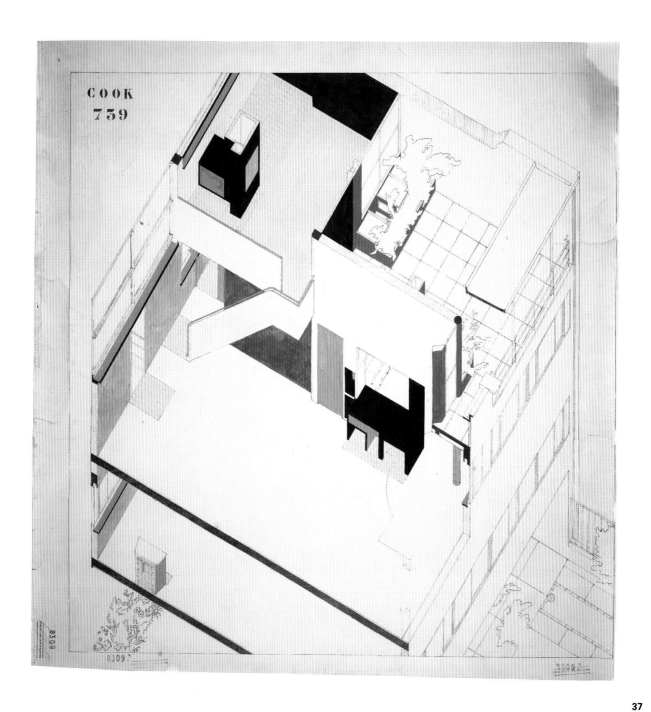

COOK
739

8309

8309

8309

37

The Rise of Modernism

By 1914, most of the elements of Modernism were in place. In 1936, the English historian Nikolaus Pevsner proclaimed: '...this new style, a genuine and adequate style of our century, was achieved by 1914' (Pevsner, p.41). But Modernism had to await the impact of the avant-garde art movements before it could achieve its characteristic forms. Expressionism (above all in Germany), de Stijl in Holland, Futurism in Italy, Constructivism in Russia and then in Europe mingled with outbreaks of Dada all over the Continent. These 'isms' were by no means unified in their ideas or appearance. Together, however, they provided the liberation to transform the language of modern architecture.

The avant-garde and their houses

The emergence of the Modernist house from the influence of the avant-garde art movements is reflected in three houses in particular, designed between 1923 and 1924.

The Schröder house in Utrecht was designed by the Dutch furniture designer Gerrit Rietveld for a strong-willed and independent young woman, Truus Schröder-Shräder. Married to a wealthy Catholic lawyer, she decided to rebel against the conventional lifestyle of the Dutch middle class, first by redesigning a room in their apartment and then, after the death of her husband in 1923, by creating a whole new house for herself and her three young children. Mrs Schröder saw her house as an opportunity to signal a significant change of life. Many Modernist clients turn out to have been undergoing similar life changes.

RIGHT
Gerrit Rietveld, Schröder house, 1924; axonometric drawing of the first floor
Collectie Centraal Museum, Utrecht

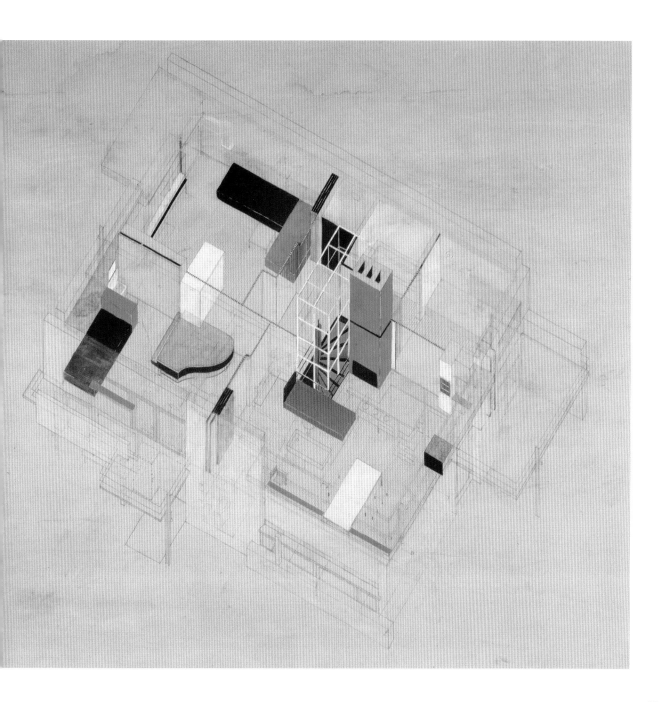

At first sight, the house is a three-dimensional de Stijl sculpture, exploding solid forms into a juxtaposition of thin planes, painted in white, grey and the three primary colours of red, yellow and blue. On the first floor, the corner which originally looked out over green fields and polders has been dissolved into two windows which can leave the angle entirely open. Inside, the whole floor can be opened out with sliding panels; closed up, individual bedrooms were provided for Mrs Schröder and her three children, each one with bed, table, chair and wash basin. Here, everything has its place, from toys and clothes to the film projector which could be wheeled out to provide proper Modernist entertainment and instruction. Countless small details show the attention paid by client and architect to using the space to best effect. This is a house which is both highly artistic and unconventional, yet intensely intimate. The very close relationship between Mrs Schröder and Rietveld, who moved into the house after his own wife died, may account for this.

ABOVE

Le Corbusier, gallery
of the La Roche house,
1923–5

Photo: Tim Benton © FLC/ ADAGP,
Paris and DACS, London 2005

LEFT

Le Corbusier, entrance
hall of the La Roche house

Photo: Tim Benton © FLC/ ADAGP,
Paris and DACS, London 2005

In 1923, the young Swiss banker Raoul La Roche asked his compatriot and friend Charles Edouard Jeanneret (Le Corbusier) to design a house 'as a frame' for his collection of Cubist and Purist artworks. The design of this house is inconceivable without the influence of the avant-garde art movements: Cubism, Purism and de Stijl.

Entering the house you step into a three-storey hall, much bigger than you could imagine from outside, into which project a balcony and a bridge which joins the two halves of the house together. The exterior seems to flow into the interior. There is a single fragile concrete post (*piloti*) supporting the first floor gallery. A sloping ramp occupies the curving wall of the gallery, whose walls are picked out in earthy colours.

RIGHT
Le Corbusier, entrance hall, La Roche house, 1923–5
Photo: Tim Benton © FLC/ ADAGP, Paris and DACS, London 2005

BELOW
Le Corbusier, entrance hall, La Roche house
Photo: Tim Benton © FLC/ ADAGP, Paris and DACS, London 2005

The house is a tour de force of surprising spatial and formal effects, but what was it like to live in? You are very aware of the hard concrete materials, on bookshelves, hand rails and ledges. Footsteps echo on the ceramic tiles in the resonant spaces. Sight is not the only or even the most important of the senses when it comes to feelings of well being. Freud argued that the sense of unease (sometimes bordering on panic), which he described as the uncanny, strikes with greatest devastation when you are at your most 'cosy'. At night the La Roche house could be a fearsome place: the large windows now black, the vast spaces virtually unlit and mysterious, the bridge across the cavernous hall vertiginous. La Roche had to cross this bridge every night on his way to bed, in a little bedroom on the third floor surrounded by the Purist paintings of his friends. Raoul La Roche loved his house and took great care of it for 43 years, until the year before his death. But it is not for everyone.

LEFT
Le Corbusier,
library of the
La Roche house,
1923–5
Photo: Tim Benton
© FLC/ ADAGP, Paris
and DACS, London 2005

ABOVE
Walter Gropius,
Georg Muche
and Adolf Meyer,
Haus am Horn,
Weimar, 1923
From M. Siebenbradt (ed.),
*Designs for the Future
Bauhaus* (2000)
© DACS 2005

LEFT
Le Corbusier,
standard house,
Pessac, 1925–6
Photo: Tim Benton
© FLC/ ADAGP,
Paris and DACS,
London 2005

Le Corbusier developed the formal idiom of his concrete houses on the back of his plans to develop 'cells' for mass housing. In 1914 he tried to patent a system for building concrete frame houses, and in 1922 he exhibited the Citrohan plaster model (see page 36). In 1925, he exhibited a full-size housing cell, the Esprit Nouveau Pavilion, which, like the Citrohan model, has a double-height living room with bedrooms on the mezzanine floor above. Comfortable English leather armchairs and cheap bentwood chairs, along with some metal tables and unit fitments, provided the only furniture. Between 1925 and 1926 Le Corbusier actually built part of a planned estate of 132 concrete houses in Pessac, a suburb of Bordeaux.

The third house, Haus am Horn, was an exhibition house, built by the Bauhaus in Weimar in 1923 to demonstrate a prototype suburban house and designed in such a way that it could be extended as a family grew. The main interest of this house, however, was the furniture and fittings provided by the Bauhaus staff and students.

The Bauhaus

The Bauhaus was founded by Walter Gropius in 1919, and dedicated to a rather mystic vision of working towards a new 'Cathedral of Socialism': painters, sculptors and craftsmen should work together to rediscover the harmony and unity of purpose of the medieval cathedral builders. The teaching started from scratch, abandoning all convention and rediscovering anew the creative potential of different materials, colours and forms. Every student had to study a foundation course (*Vorkurs*) in which exercises of this kind were carried out, and when they progressed to the workshops they continued to receive separate 'form' instruction in parallel to their technical training. This preparation helped Bauhaus designers to rethink design fundamentally and arrive at quite new forms.

The Hungarian craftsman Marcel Breuer, who designed much of the furniture for the exhibition house, had been a student at the Bauhaus before being taken on as a master. His wooden chair, while still firmly within the hand craftsmanship tradition, betrays the curiosity to explore the potential of cantilevering beyond vertical supports, which derived from experimenting with the structural potential of materials in the Bauhaus *Vorkurs*.

ABOVE
Eric Mendelsohn,
Sternfeld house,
Berlin, 1922
Photo: Charlotte Benton

LEFT
Marcel Breuer,
Lath chair.
Polished cherry
wood, webbing
and fabric. 1922
V&A: W.6–1988

A similar search to express the structural rationale of the new materials, while using conventional construction, can be seen in Eric Mendelsohn's Sternfeld house. The dramatic effect of appearing to cantilever large slabs of the house is simulated by the use of strips of dark brick which group the windows together. These tricks would disappear once the materials and know-how made real cantilevers possible, using steel or reinforced concrete construction.

In 1923, many of the Bauhaus designs betrayed the de Stijl influence of Van Doesburg, who set up his own studio in Weimar and attracted many of the Bauhaus students to follow his courses. The cradle by Peter Keler not only uses the de Stijl primary colours, but refers to a study by the painter Wassily Kandinsky and his students to establish whether there was a relationship between the primary colours and the primary geometric shapes of circle, square and triangle.

Two years later, Breuer began to design in a more 'modern' material, tubular steel, supposedly after learning to ride a bicycle in Dessau. His 'Wassily' chair (so-called in the 1960s because Wassily Kandinsky owned one) translated the padded forms of a leather armchair into lines of force spanned by strips of leather. It was a symbolic act of stripping away bourgeois comfort to reveal both the structural and useful elements in their purest form. Breuer set up the firm Standard Möbel, with Kalman Lengyel, to manufacture tubular steel furniture, and soon it seemed that every modern architect had to design cantilevered chairs. Using the in-built resilience of high-performance cold drawn steel tubing to create a sturdy frame with the appearance of a single loop of tubing was a classic Modernist design problem. Mies was the first to patent the principle of the cantilever chair, although this patent was later challenged.

LEFT
Charlotte Perriand,
revolving chair.
Tubular steel and
leather upholstery.
1928
V&A: W.35–1987
© DACS 2005

In France, designers were quick to follow the trend. Charlotte Perriand worked with Le Corbusier for ten years from 1927, and used her experience as a professional furniture designer to add a touch of leather-upholstered luxury to her designs, while Jean Prouvé chose to use stamped sheet steel in his highly inventive designs.

Tubular steel furniture came to be one of the most potent icons of Modernism. Parodied as 'chaste' by Heath Robinson, it was frequently used to symbolize 'modern' morals, as in Noël Coward's play *Private Lives*, in September 1930, when some of the first tubular steel chairs and tables to be seen in London were used to accompany the flirtations on stage at the Phoenix Theatre.

One of the most brilliant of the Bauhaus students, Marianne Brandt, later taken on as teaching staff, managed to combine the study of pure forms potentially suitable for mass production while executing the highest standard of metalworking craftsmanship. She gradually moved from forms only suitable for hand manufacture to objects which could actually be mass produced, such as lighting fittings. Naum Slutzky was another experienced metalworker in the Weimar Bauhaus, designing silverware and jewellery which absorbed Bauhaus formal imagery but remained firmly in the realm of craftsmanship.

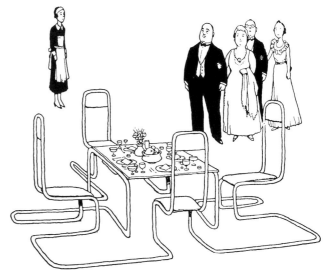

The one-piece chromium steel dining suite

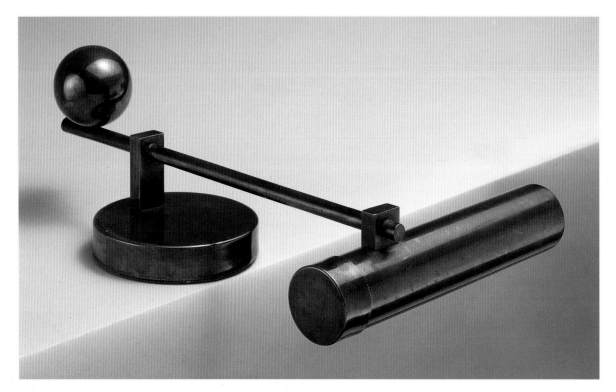

ABOVE
J.J.P. Oud, Giso 404 piano lamp.
Lacquered patinated brass.
c.1928.

The Metropolitan Museum of Art,
Purchase, Charina Foundation Inc.
Gift, 2002. (2002.16) Photograph © 2002
The Metropolitan Museum of Art.
© DACS 2005

RIGHT
Poul Henningsen,
table lamp.
Nickel-plated brass,
Bakelite, aluminium
and white opalescent
glass. 1928
V&A: M. 26:1-5–1992

Walter Gropius put on an exhibition of architectural photographs and models on the occasion of the Haus am Horn exhibition, which drew together international examples of Modernism from America, Germany, Austria, France and central Europe. Later published as *Internationale Architektur* (1925), this volume represented most of the designs in the form of drawings or models, since little had as yet been constructed.

Meanwhile, the prototypes of modern product design were emerging from the Bauhaus, where, from 1923, the emphasis was increasingly on industrial design, and from other centres of Modernism.

Designing an electric lamp which owed nothing to spirit lamps or gas chandeliers occupied many Modernist designers. The Danish designer and critic Poul Henningsen patented his system of concentric, carefully profiled shades, and his lamps were widely admired. J.J.P. Oud designed a piano lamp for a friend, an ingenious play with tubes and spheres. This design was taken up and adapted by the Dutch firm Gispen, which also manufactured and sold lighting fittings by Henningsen and others.

The experiments with unlikely combinations of materials and colours in the Bauhaus textile workshops led to highly innovative designs. Gunta Stölzl used new materials such as cellophane and raffia in her furnishing textiles. Her decorative pieces are suffused with the bright colour and carefully modulated tones learned from the painter Paul Klee, who taught on the preliminary course at the Bauhaus. The sale of wallhangings and wallpapers were among the school's less glamorous but most influential successes after the Bauhaus's move to the city of Dessau.

International Modernism

From 1926 to 1933, Modernist houses were designed and built all over
Europe, sharing a basic approach but differing in appearance.

Mies designed his Tugendhat house in Brno, Czechoslovakia, with plate
glass windows which could disappear completely into the floor. The
purism and austerity of the interior is mitigated by the use of luxurious
marble surfaces.

In Paris, the French furniture designer Pierre Chareau teamed up with
the avant-garde Dutch architect Bijvoet to design an extraordinary house
for the gynaecologist Dalsace. A double height living space is faced
entirely in glass bricks, designed to be illuminated at night by
searchlights outside. Ingenious metal alloy cupboards and an abundance
of bathrooms and hand basins give the house the quality of a bizarre
invention. To speed the arrival of hot food from the kitchen, an over-head
railway was designed with a dumb waiter which was meant to deliver
dishes direct to the dining table.

In Holland, Modernism took a generally austere and functional form. The architects Brinkman and Van der Vlught built one of the icons of Modernism in Europe, the Van Nelle factory near Rotterdam (see page 29), while the interiors of the houses they built for Kees van der Leeuw and Bertus Sonneveld (both directors of the Van Nelle factory) were brightly coloured but hard as nails on the surface.

The German architect Hans Scharoun designed a number of houses in a more or less Expressionist idiom before creating one of the most exotic of the Modernist houses. The Schminke house responds to the site and its garden both on the exterior, where a jutting balcony over-flies a small pool, and on the interior, where a sloping wall of glass creates an exotic winter garden full of tropical plants.

The Irish Art Deco designer Eileen Gray began to turn towards Modernist design after she came to know the Rumanian architect and critic Jean Badovici, and together they designed an experimental house on rocks overlooking the Mediterranean near Nice. Every detail of life was studied and furniture designed around precise daily routines. Cupboards and drawers had the names of their contents stencilled onto them; everything had its place, as on a yacht.

It might be thought that Eileen Gray, as a female designer, would be more interested in comfort than some of her male colleagues, but this was not the case. Her folding armchair was inspired by deck chairs on ocean liners and, although beautifully made and conceived, is not particularly comfortable. Bathroom, kitchen and the various sleeping areas are small and austere, to allow maximum space for the main reception rooms. But Gray's attention to purely personal needs stands in opposition to the attempt to design for universal needs and mass markets, to which most modern designers aspired.

As in the case of tubular steel furniture, a rapid and vigorous plagiarism ensured that ingenious modern designs quickly spread throughout Europe. For example, Wilhelm Wagenfeld, a student at the Weimar Bauhaus before setting up his own practice, designed a glass tea service which was soon copied in Czechoslovakia and elsewhere.

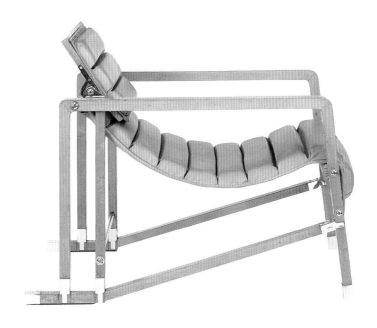

ABOVE
Eileen Gray, prototype
folding armchair. Sycamore
frame, chronium plated
mounts and fixtures, leather
upholstery. 1925

FAR LEFT
Ladislav Sutnar, tea set.
Heat-resistant glass,
steel, wood. 1931
The Museum of
Decorative Arts, Prague

LEFT
Wilhelm Wagenfeld, tea
service. Mould-blown,
heat resistant glass.1931
V&A Museum
© DACS 2005

Housing the masses

Underlying Modernism in architecture was the commitment to resolve the problems of mass housing and the city. In some cities, such as Rotterdam, Berlin and Frankfurt, Modernist architects were placed in charge of major rehousing projects. J.J.P. Oud designed a number of estates in Rotterdam, at a rock-bottom level of amenity (no bath or shower) but providing clean, light and airy interiors for the thousands of rural immigrants flocking to the city. The Kiefhoek estate was frequently illustrated and much admired for the clarity of the overall conception and the ingenious planning of the interiors. Traces of influence from Oud's de Stijl background can be seen in the colour scheme in his photomontage. Although the yellow and green colours shown here were not executed, the bright red front doors were included.

LEFT
Ernst May,
Höhenblick estate,
Ginsberger Hang,
Frankfurt, 1925–6
Photo: Charlotte Benton

His colleague Cornelis van Eesteren also included pure de Stijl colours
in some of his work, such as his design for a street of houses and shops.
In Frankfurt, Ernst May and a team of architects and designers built the
single most consistent and extensive development of workers' housing
between 1925 and 1930, which they publicized vigorously in a magazine
called *Das Neue Frankfurt*. Divided into impressive multi-storey
apartment blocks framing the main intersections, and modest terraced
houses with gardens, the estates were laid out along the banks of the
Nidda river, on sites prudently reserved for expansion by the city fathers
before the war.

May called in a number of architects and designers to equip his workers'
housing. Ferdinand Kramer designed everything from cheap but robust
bentwood chairs to stoves and cupboards, which were manufactured
and used in thousands of apartments, as well as being marketed
externally. Standard plans and details were used in the Frankfurt housing
estates, including those for kitchens and bathrooms.

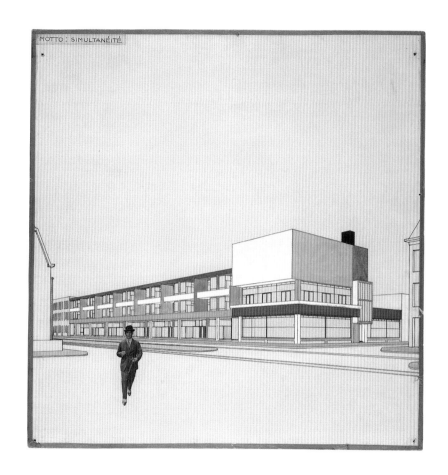

MOTTO : SIMULTANÉITÉ

Cornelis van Eesteren,
Competition design for a
shopping street with housing
above in Den Haag, 1924.

Nederlands Architectuurinstituut,
Rotterdam/collection Van Eesteren-Fluck
& Van Lohuizen foundation, The Hague.
Archive: Van Eesteren. Inv.nr.: III.250

Margarete Schütte-Lihotzky designed a 'minimal' kitchen for use in the Frankfurt housing settlements that was imitated all over Europe. The original was equipped with a moveable over-head light, a so-called Norwegian stove (a well-insulated box which would allow food to cook slowly during the day), built-in glass storage drawers and work surfaces calculated for efficient food preparation. In a slightly larger version, used in the Höhenblick estate, Frankfurt, Schütte-Lihotzky provided a corner in which the housewife or cook could sit.

The study of the kitchen as a work place began in America with the work of Catherine Beecher and Christine Frederick and quickly spread to Europe. Erna Meyer in Germany, Paulette de Bernège in France and Mrs Darcy Braddell in Britain waged parallel campaigns to make kitchens better suited to domestic labour and comfort. Popular annual exhibitions, such as the Salon des Arts Ménagers in Paris and the Ideal Home exhibitions in London, maintained interest in this research.

Development went along two apparently contradictory lines. Many people wanted a large kitchen as the centre of family life where meals could be taken except on formal occasions. However, architects and health inspectors involved in housing redevelopment were against the large kitchen-living room, which they considered unhygienic. Kitchens were either located as a niche off the living room or packed into the smallest possible space, in imitation of the tiny galleys on express trains.

Many architects turned their hand to kitchen design, and Le Corbusier won many clients through the popularity of his kitchens. The Belgian Modernist L.H. de Koninck actually stole one of Le Corbusier's clients when he built the Canneel house in 1930; he later specialized in designing modular fitments for kitchens, which acquired considerable cachet under the name Cubex.

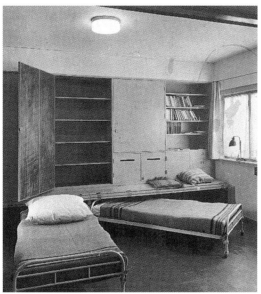

ABOVE
Franz Singer,
apartment design
Bauhaus Archiv, Berlin

The bedroom too came under scrutiny in these housing estates. Folding beds could be used to make more space available in the daytime. One of the demonstration apartments at Frankfurt, designed by Margarete Schütte-Lihotzky and her husband, featured beds which folded away in a cupboard, thus allowing a single room to serve different functions by day and night.

Franz Singer, an Austrian designer and architect, also specialized in ingenious arrangements, in which beds slid out from underneath platforms, chairs folded away under counters and tables extended from nowhere.

Weissenhof Siedlung

The aspirations of mass housing and the ambitions of Modernist architects were brought together in the Weissenhof exhibition of demonstration houses in Stuttgart in 1927.

This was an international exhibition, promoted by the German *Werkbund* (the German equivalent of the British Design and Industries Association) under the leadership of Mies van der Rohe, who invited Modernist architects from all over Europe to take part. The dwellings were meant to incorporate new materials and suggest prototypes for mass housing. Le Corbusier built a full-size version of the Citrohan building he had exhibited as a model in 1922, Mies built a small block of flats, Gropius a prefabricated house in steel.

J.J.P. Oud, with his wide experience as a housing designer, made the best attempt to design realistic housing. On the street side of his row of houses, a metal door, which could be opened remotely from the kitchen, gave access to a little courtyard housing a shed for a bicycle or pram and coals. The kitchen was designed along the latest principles to allow a housewife to sit while preparing food, minimizing the movements required while preparing a meal. A hatch allowed food to be passed directly to the living room.

Oud's compatriot Mart Stam also designed a group of terraced houses, based on a steel frame construction. Adolf Rading's and Hans Scharoun's houses were more elaborate, both involving the use of folding screens to open up or subdivide the space in the manner pioneered by Gerrit Rietveld in the Schröder house.

Bathrooms and bedrooms were also studied with a view to minimizing space used and maximizing convenience. Le Corbusier's own bedroom and bathroom in his studio apartment featured a tubular steel bed cemented into the wall (high enough to look out over Paris), with a built-in lamp, mirror and ventilator by the side of the bed. The shower was next to the bed, while the hand basin was lit by a panel of glass tiles.

Once again, this is not everyone's idea of comfort, but curiously satisfying aesthetically. The kitchen, however, was designed for his wife Yvonne and was much admired, with its convenient cupboards and hammered zinc surfaces imitating the traditional French café.

Promoting Modernism

Housing exhibitions followed in Breslau (1928), Vienna (1931), and in many other cities. These helped to promote public interest in Modernism. In addition, a stream of books and magazine articles began to appear after 1925, promoting the virtues of Modernist design for private architecture and for 'minimal' housing. The Czech architect and critic Karel Teige wrote one of the most impassioned of these books, *Minimum Dwelling*, arguing for a collectivization of most aspects of family life in housing blocks where the preparation of food, laundry and care of children would be dealt with communally.

The first full conference of the CIAM (International Congresses of Modern Architecture) met in Frankfurt in 1929 to examine the problem of the 'minimal existence' dwelling. Hundreds of floor plans, all drawn to the same scale and to the same convention, compared practice across Europe. Almost all these plans were for apartments or terraced houses. In Continental Europe, where urban dwellers had always lived largely in multi-occupancy tenement buildings, the reform of the apartment plan was accepted with equanimity. Many Modernist housing estates were provided with collective clothes washing facilities, crèches and even schools, but the replacement of home dinners by collective canteens did not take on.

In Britain, the move to house people in flats was not accepted so easily, and the vast majority of the rehousing programme between the wars took the form of semi-detached or terraced houses.

LEFT
Karel Teige, book cover
of *Minimum Dwelling*,
1932
Museum of Decorative
Arts in Prague

The Warming of Modernism

By 1929, images and details of Modernist houses had been published in books and journals all over the world. As different countries engaged with Modernism, its forms diversified. Some architects softened their work with brick and stone and natural planting; others exaggerated even further the transparent and mechanical. In countries like Britain and Hungary, dominated by traditionalist architects, Modernism was practised by the young in defiance of the established institutions. In countries like Holland, Czechoslovakia and Germany, Modernism became accepted in many quarters as a general practice. By 1939, Modernism was effectively an optional style available to the house builder in most countries.

Leading Modernist architects had begun to turn away from the colder, more functionalist aspects of Modernism since at least 1930. The Russian-born architect Berthold Lubetkin designed some of the purest expressions of Modernist architecture in Britain, but by the time he came to design his own penthouse apartment in 1937–8, his approach had changed. He included a pale blue vaulted ceiling to soften the light, and brown tiles on the floor. His armchairs were designed with only one arm, to encourage the sitter to sprawl across the chair.

LEFT
Berthold Lubetkin,
interior of
penthouse at
Highpoint II, 1937–8

LEFT
Alvar Aalto,
armchair. Birch
plywood and solid
birch, painted seat.
1930
V&A: W.14–1987

ABOVE
'Functional' in Osbert
Lancaster, *Homes Sweet
Homes*, 1939

BELOW
Marcel Breuer, Long
chair (short version).
Moulded birch plywood
with zebrano veneer.
1936
V&A: Circ.80–1975

Modernist designers all over Europe also began to soften the hard lines and textures of Modernism. A sign of this was the sudden interest in wooden furniture. Osbert Lancaster, sensitive barometer to the changing mood, reflects this perfectly in his 1930s English Modernist interior. The German tubular steel furniture is left out on the veranda in the rain, while modern man enjoys his pipe on an Alvar Aalto stool, with the promise of an Aalto armchair and the comfort of a few abstract paintings and even a plant (albeit a prickly one).

The display object had been banished by hard-line Modernists in the 1920s, but it began to make a comeback in the 1930s. Not of course the miscellaneous *objets d'art* of the old generation, but *objets à reaction poétique*: works of curious natural beauty picked up on the beach or while hiking, and capable of stimulating the artist's imagination.

The Finnish architect Alvar Aalto set the scene with his bentwood chairs, manufactured in Finland and exported with great success in England through the firm Finmar. An English businessman, Jack Pritchard, set up a company, Isokon, to manufacture and market modern wooden furniture; this was the route to English affections. Marcel Breuer, pioneer of steel furniture in the 1920s, turned to wooden furniture on emigrating to England in 1933, while an inventive English designer, Gerald Summer, also designed his own wooden furniture, trying to find ways of folding and cutting single sheets of plywood to make a viable industrial product. In this he was following the Dutch designer Gerrit Rietveld, who had carried out similar experiments using the rather more malleable material of fibreboard.

Other Modernist architects developed their own more humanistic approach in the 1930s. Hans Scharoun stayed on in Germany during the National Socialist period (despite the persecution and exile of most of his friends) and managed to continue working on a series of houses, whose astonishingly inventive interiors were disguised behind conventional brick street façades. The plans open out into curving shapes on different levels, affording a range of views of the garden and seeming to bring the landscape into the house. Many German architects, such as Eric Mendelsohn and Hans Scharoun, had talked about 'organic' architecture, and these houses come as close as anything to exemplifying these ideas.

A common feature of Modernist houses in the 1930s was the use of natural flagstones which ran uninterrupted from exterior veranda to interior living room. Architects discovered that they could reap the benefits of using natural materials – brick, stone and wood – while still introducing the open spaces and generous expanses of glass which demonstrated the separation of structure from enclosure and which defined Modernism in architecture.

In America, the tradition of organic architecture promoted by the brilliant Frank Lloyd Wright merged with the ideas of two Austrian émigrés, who sought out Wright on their arrival in the US and learned from him. For Wright, architecture should appear to grow naturally from the site, and his ideas had influenced many European architects since 1908, when two books of his work had been published in Germany. The Austrian architect Richard Neutra kept in contact with the avant-garde European circles even after moving to Los Angeles, as did his young associate Schindler, who worked on Wright's Hollyhock house in Los Angeles before setting up practice on his own there.

The house designed by Rudolf Schindler for himself and his wife Pauline, and for another family, Clyde and Marian Chace, combined five studio spaces for sleeping and working arranged around a central utility area.

Meanwhile, Neutra designed one of the best publicized and most admired American Modernist houses for a health fanatic, Dr Lovell. Perched high on a ravine, the Lovell Health house touches the landscape as lightly as possible, supported on thin steel stanchions. The interior incorporates very large open spaces on different levels. When Schindler poached Lovell for a more modest beach house at Newport, Neutra was not amused.

Schindler had a reciprocal influence on Frank Lloyd Wright, whose Falling Water is among the most European of his 1930s houses. Reinforced concrete is expressively used by Wright to cantilever large balconies over the stream which gives the house its name.

But it was the Finnish architect Alvar Aalto who designed the house which most perfectly expresses the longing to combine modernity with natural materials and processes. His Villa Mairea is set in virgin forest and deploys a series of unexpected and complex spaces.

Modernism on Trial

So was Modernism a great mistake perpetrated by over-zealous architects on an unsuspecting and reluctant world? During the late 1960s and 1970s the confidence in Modernism as an idea came unpicked. This was partly because of the stampede to build shoddy Modernist tower blocks in the rush to reconstruct after the war, and partly because Modernist ideas became clichés. Quantity not quality wins votes. But it is difficult to over-emphasize how Modernism has changed our world, from plate glass windows to flat-packed furniture, from white painted interiors to glass teapots, from wooden stools to tubular steel chairs. Despite the rejection of the excesses of doctrinaire Modernism, many of its products and fundamental principles are part of every home.

To love Modernism, you have to be inspired by its hope for the future and its belief in the power of the imagination. When Le Corbusier designed a tiny guest bedroom for himself and his wife in his mother's house, he invented a monastic reading place for himself, raised on a block so that he could see out over Lake Geneva. This is the essential Modernist home reduced to the minimum: a bed, a table and chair, and a beautiful view.

Further Reading

Banham, R., *Theory and Design in the First Machine Age* (London, 1960)

Bertram, A., *The House: A Machine for Living In. A summary of the art and science of homemaking considered functionally* (London, 1935)

Geest, J. v. and Macel, O., *Stühle aus Stahl* (Cologne, 1981)

Giedion, S., *Buildings in France (Bauten in Frankreich)* (Santa Monica, California, 1995)

Gropius, W., *Internationale Architektur* (Munich, 1925)

Hitchcock, H.-R. and Johnson, P., *The International Style: Architecture since 1922* (New York, 1966)

Neumeyer, F., *The Artless Word; Mies van der Rohe on the Building Art* (Cambridge, Massachusetts, 1991)

Pevsner, N., *Pioneers of the Modern Movement* (London, 1936)

Risselada, M. (ed.), *Functionalisme 1927–1961, Hans Scharoun versus de Opbouw* (Delft, 1997)

Robinson, H., *How to Live in a Flat* (London, 1936)

Solà-Morales, I., Cirici, C. and Ramos, F., *Mies van der Rohe, El Pabellon de Barcelona* (Barcelona, 1993)

Taut, B., *Modern Architecture* (London, 1929)

Taut, B., *Die Neue Baukunst in Europa und Amerika* (1979)

Tinniswood, A., *The Art Deco House: Avant-garde houses of the 1920s and 1930s* (London, 2002)

Weston, R., *Villa Mairea* (London, 1992)

Index

Page numbers in italic refer to
the illustrations on those pages